Contents

Page references in these Notes are to the Heinemann
Educational edition of *A Man for All Seasons*, but as Act
references are also given, the Notes may be used
with any edition of the book.

Preface by the general editor

The intention throughout this study aid is to stimulate and guide, to encourage your involvement in the book, and to develop informed responses and a sure understanding of the main details.

Brodie's Notes provide a clear outline of the play or novel's plot, followed by act, scene, or chapter summaries and/or commentaries. These are designed to emphasize the most important literary and factual details. Poems, stories or non-fiction texts combine brief summary with critical commentary on individual aspects or common features of the genre being examined. Textual notes define what is difficult or obscure and emphasize literary qualities. Revision questions are set at appropriate points to test your ability to appreciate the prescribed book and to write accurately and relevantly about it.

In addition, each of these Notes includes a critical appreciation of the author's art. This covers such major elements as characterization, style, structure, setting and themes. Poems are examined technically – rhyme, rhythm, for instance. In fact, any important aspect of the prescribed work will be evaluated. The aim is to send you back to the text you are studying.

Each study aid concludes with a series of general questions which require a detailed knowledge of the book: some of these questions may invite comparison with other books, some will be suitable for coursework exercises, and some could be adapted to work you are doing on another book or books. Each study aid has been adapted to meet the needs of the current examination requirements. They provide a basic, individual and imaginative response to the work being studied, and it is hoped that they will stimulate you to acquire disciplined reading habits and critical fluency.

Graham Handley 1991

To the student

A close reading of the play is the student's primary task, but if you can see a performance of the play or film this too would be helpful. These Notes will help to increase your understanding and appreciation of the work, and to stimulate *your own* thinking about it: *they are in no way intended as a substitute* for a thorough knowledge of the play.

The author and his work

Robert Oxton Bolt was born at Sale, Cheshire, on 15 August 1924, the son of Ralph Bolt and his wife Leah. He was educated at Manchester Grammar School, which has given so many remarkable men to public life. But young Bolt as a schoolboy does not seem to have made the most of his early opportunities, and in 1941 he left school to become an office boy in the Sun Life Assurance Office (thereby recalling the first steps of two other English playwrights, John Drinkwater and R. C. Sherriff, who first made their careers in insurance).

Bolt did not spend long in the insurance business, and in 1943 he enrolled at Manchester University, but he was now of an age when enlistment in the Forces in World War II was obligatory. In the three years until 1946 he served in various places, including France. On his demobilization he returned to Manchester University for three years. Then he completed a post-graduate course at Exeter University in 1950.

On leaving the university he immediately took up school-teaching as a career, first at a village school in Bishopsteignton, Devon, and later as teacher of English Literature at Millfield School, Somerset, where he remained until 1958. He then gave up teaching for the uncertainties of freelance writing.

He wrote several radio and television features and his experience with the BBC quickly established his claim to be one of the coming young men. His first play in the live theatre was *The Critic and the Hearth*, which was produced at the Oxford Playhouse. Almost immediately the script of *Flowering Cherry* was accepted by a famous company in the West End, and was put on at the Haymarket Theatre, London, where it met with instant success. The play had a similar success in America at the Lyceum Theatre, New York.

Probably a good deal of the play's success was due to a first-class production and the acting of Sir Ralph Richardson; but Bolt again succeeded with his next play, *A Man for All Seasons*, which was produced in the West End, this time at the Globe Theatre, London. Once more in New York the work of the rising playwright met with an enthusiastic reception.

Robert Brustein, drama critic of *The New Republic*, Professor of English Literature at Columbia University and Dean of the School of Drama at Yale, explained the attraction of the play when he commented, 'Compared with the historical plays of Anouilh and Osborne, it shows remarkable intelligence, historicity, theatrical ingenuity and good taste. I confess the work took me by surprise, for nothing in the *Flowering Cherry* prepared me for the kind of form and substance he handles with such authority here.'

In 1960, the year of *A Man for All Seasons*' production, another play of Bolt's appeared: *The Tiger and the Horse*, which had its première at the Queen's Theatre, London.

Bolt next turned his attention to film scripts, and his *Lawrence of Arabia* won the British Film Academy Award for 1962. Bolt was also responsible for the scenario and script of the film adaptation of Boris Pasternak's *Dr Zhivago* in 1965. Then followed the film version of *A Man for All Seasons*, Bolt's own adaptation of the play. The film gained a Hollywood Oscar for the best film play of 1966 and the British Film Academy Award for the same year. Awards were also made to Paul Scofield for best actor of the year, and to the director Fred Zinnemann. Bolt's next two films appeared in 1970 (*Ryan's Daughter*) and 1972 (*Lady Caroline Lamb*).

After the play of *A Man for All Seasons*, three more plays by Bolt appeared: *Gentle Jack* in 1963; *The Thwarting of Baron Bolligrew* (for children) in 1965; and *Vivat! Vivat Regina!* in 1970.

Bolt has been fortunate in his interpreters; the country's leading stars – Ralph Richardson, Michael Redgrave, Edith Evans, Paul Scofield and others have appeared, ably supported by some of the foremost actors of the period.

Bolt is one of the new dramatists that have revolutionized the theatre in the mid twentieth century. The première of John Osborne's *Look Back in Anger* on 8 May 1956 marked the beginning of a new era in British drama. The great days of the theatrical renaissance, the days of Shaw and Galsworthy, had given way to the rather artificial products of Frederick Lonsdale, Nöel Coward, Terence Rattigan and a host of minor writers who largely catered for the fashionable 'West End Theatre', that square mile of theatrical London within the area of Shaftesbury Avenue, Drury Lane and Covent Garden; there the fare was pretty much 'the mixture as before'. Occasionally it threw up a *bravura* writer like Christopher Fry, whose *The Lady's not for Burning* is the all-time model for theatrical pyrotechnics, a mixture of whimsy, colour and verbal cadenzas. But generally the West End theatre played to a formula that James Bridie wittily defined as 'two hours amidst the erotic misadventures of the English upper classes'.

For years the greatest figures in English literature – men like James Joyce, Yeats and their equals – had turned their backs on this type of theatre, with its vacuous audiences. Somerset Maugham had abandoned play-writing in despair.

Exactly what caused the sudden flurry, the excitement, the new life is uncertain. Possibly producers like George Devine and Joan Littlewood were responsible. Whatever the cause, good writers suddenly found that they were welcome in the new theatre. The theatre had become liberated. In quick succession playwrights like Arnold Wesker, Brendan Behan, Sheila Delaney, John Whiting, John Arden, Harold Pinter and Samuel Beckett emerged. The avant-garde of Continental writers made their appearance – Bertolt Brecht, Friedrich Dürrenmatt, Ionesco, Max Frisch, Albert Camus, Ugo Betti and others.

Fresh actors with new styles emerged. No longer was it essential to copy Gielgud and Olivier. The new stage had for its heroes actors like Paul Scofield, Leo McKern, Alan Bates, Alan Dobie, Richard Pascoe, Albert Finney, Peter O'Toole; and producers like Peter Hall came to the fore. The mannered style of acting that saw its heyday in such performers as Rex Harrison, Ray Milland and Nöel Coward gave way to the proletarian manliness of 'Actors in the Raw'. Well might the dowager in the stalls exclaim, 'I never knew till now that Shakespeare's Romans spoke with a Liverpool accent.'

It was all part of the theatrical shake-up, and suddenly all the old stereotyped conventions and artificialities of the fashionable West End theatre gave way: Jimmy Porter's jazz trumpet blew away the old colonels and frowsy upper-class hangers on. The genteel accents, the 'posh' shibboleths faded overnight and all we seemed to hear in the theatre was the Cockney soldier in Behan's *Hostage* crying, 'O Death Where is thy Sting-a-ling-a-ling?'

The most important aspect of this revolution in taste was that it was genuine and real – it was not a palace revolution. For centuries the theatre had been the closely-guarded citadel, the preserve of the privileged few. It seemed that after 1956 the Bastille had fallen – and the stage was occupied by the works of new young dramatists. It was in this atmosphere that Robert Bolt first found success.

Historical background

Life of Sir Thomas More

Thomas More was born in the city of London on 6 February 1478, the second child in a middle-class family: his father John More was butler and steward at Lincoln's Inn, and in 1517 became a judge in the Court of King's Bench. John More died in 1530, only five years before his son's downfall.

Thomas went to St Anthony's School, Threadneedle Street (1486), where he first learned the Latin for which he was renowned, and in which he was later to write one of the world's greatest documents – *Utopia* (1516). One must never forget that his own instruction followed the pattern of the age of chivalry; and his education owes much to the fact that as a boy he was sent to the household of Cardinal Morton, at that time Lord Chancellor of England. There he learned the arts proper to a gentleman; and he early attracted notice: Cardinal Morton would often say to guests at table, 'Mark that lad, one day he will prove a marvellous man.'

On the recommendation of Morton, More was sent in 1492 to Canterbury Hall, Oxford (later absorbed in Christ Church College). We do not know precisely who his tutors were, though it is generally supposed that he learned Greek under Grocyn, and from Linacre. Certainly the climate of culture was that of the New Learning, and More's father was afraid that his son was going to be influenced by the new ideas, to the extent that he might well abandon the Law, which had been chosen as his career. Thomas was therefore recalled to London, where his father could supervise his studies.

Thomas was entered at an Inn of Chancery, and soon made his mark in law. He prospered so well that almost as soon as he was called to the bar he was appointed reader (i.e. lecturer or tutor) in law to the Faculty of Furnival's Inn. He did not neglect his literary, philosophical and theological studies, however, for while still in his early twenties he delivered a series of lectures on St Augustine in Dr Grocyn's church of St Laurence, Old Jewry. It was during this period that he became a friend of the world-famous Dutch-born humanist and scholar, Erasmus (Desiderius

Erasmus, 1466–1536). In 1499 Erasmus paid his first visit to England and by the end of the year their friendship was firmly cemented.

As a young man, More desired to enter the Church. For years he considered becoming a monk; and, indeed, until the last he used to mortify his flesh and wear a hair-shirt. (This shirt was said to be one of the relics treasured by the Augustines of Abbot's Leigh in Somerset.) Finally he decided against a monastic vocation: to use the words of Erasmus, he preferred to be a chaste husband rather than an impure monk. (The period of this dedication to a monkish life was 1499 to 1503.)

In 1504 he was elected to Parliament, and the following year he married; his first marriage was short lived, lasting only four years; after his wife's death he remarried – and it is this second wife Alice who figures in the play by Robert Bolt. 1509, the year of Henry VIII's accession to the throne, was the beginning of More's rise to eminence.

At first he acquired fame as a pleader or advocate in the courts; he was soon earning substantial sums, and his income has been estimated at the equivalent of £200,000 of today's money. In short, he was clearly established as one of the leaders of the Bar. He was soon elected Bencher of Lincoln's Inn, and in 1510 became the Under-Sheriff of the City of London. He was engaged as one of the counsel in a famous suit against the Crown and attracted the attention of the young King. He was soon pressed into the King's service, at first as Ambassador to Flanders, in which post he soon satisfied Wolsey that he possessed an alert brain and considerable ability for undertaking matters of state.

In 1516 More wrote *Utopia*; and in the same year his friendship with Henry VIII began to ripen. Henry was at this time not the gross despot of later years but a handsome young prince who took all knowledge for his province: a fluent linguist; an expert on the lute and harpsichord; a capable athlete – in short a promising philosopher-king, truly a monarch. And he passionately identified himself with the New Learning and all it implied.

In the light of what we now know, we are inclined to look upon More's early relationship with Henry as something of an intellectual trap. With the hindsight of history, we think of More as the intellectual companion of Erasmus: in fact he was the everyday friend of the rising young prince; they enjoyed each other's company and spent hours in argument and discussion. Not that More was deceived by the friendship of great princes. 'The king walks arm-in-arm with me. But I have no cause to be proud. For if my head would win him a castle in France, it should not fail to go.' Clearly, More was under no illusions, as this remark to Roper, his son-in-law, shows.

The King was a frequent guest in More's home at Chelsea – a mansion bought in 1523. He often dined there, without notice, and shared something of More's family life. It is interesting to recall that in this very family circle, where the King was a frequent 'friend of the family', the youngest daughter Cecily later married a man who was to become foreman of the jury that sent Anne Boleyn to the block. As one of More's biographers remarks, this was surely a coincidence no historical novelist would dream of contriving!

In 1529, Wolsey, the most hated man in England, fell from power; and the land rejoiced. Thomas More had served under him, and had a thorough knowledge of the circumstances that had laid Wolsey low. More was created Lord Chancellor in his place – the first layman in England ever to become Lord Chancellor – 'Keeper of The Conscience of the King'. With this appointment the vested interest in the King's affairs by the Church was arrested. The choice was popular – More was known as a ceaseless critic of corruption; as a judge he had never been known to take a bribe. He was the natural man to call on. He justified the choice, and for the first time the business of the courts was despatched with regularity and utter fairness.

Soon after More had taken up office, the King's pressure began to be exercised. He dearly wanted the divorce that Wolsey had failed to negotiate. The Lord Chancellor entreated the King to forgive him. From that moment More was at variance with the King's policy and he in turn was doomed. Realizing More would not yield, the King was forced to choose other advisers. His eye turned on Thomas Cromwell, a crafty and calculating disciple of Machiavelli who bore no love for More. It is not necessary for our purpose to trace the steps which led to More's forfeiting the Great Seal. It is sufficient to note that in 1532 he left office a poor man – a fact that speaks eloquently of his incorruptibility. He was voted a sum of £5,000 in recognition of his work – which he declined. Yet if he thought to avoid a cruel fate, he was mistaken. Henry held the view that 'he that is not with me is against me'. More's absence from the Coronation of Anne Boleyn as Queen was carefully noted by both Cromwell and his royal master. From that moment the contest became a matter of personal rancour and intrigue.

The first signs were manifest in an attempt to charge More with accepting bribes. But the circumstances were so well known, and More was so obviously incorruptible, that this charge was refuted almost as soon as it was made.

Again More realized that his enemy would never be satisfied till his head rolled in the dust. 'What is postponed is not finished,' he told his daughter Margaret. In March 1534 a bill made the authority of the Pope in England invalid, and everyone was called upon to take an oath of Supremacy – to the effect that Henry, and not the Pope or his Deputy, was head of the Church. It was this that More refused to acknowledge. As a lawyer, he took refuge in every legal defence that he could – but he would not take a spurious oath.

Persisting in his refusal, More was committed to the Tower on 17 April 1534. The proceedings dragged on until July 1535, when he was tried before a packed jury at Westminster Hall. Even then the Crown had to rely on the evidence of perjured testimony – the perjurer was Rich, the very man who in his younger days had been helped by More. As a result of this perjury, More was found guilty of treason and was duly executed on 7 July 1535. His judicial murder did not satisfy the Defender of the Faith, Henry VIII. The small property that More left was confiscated, and his widow was driven from her home. Every penny was settled on the Princess Elizabeth, daughter of Anne Boleyn, who grimly held on to the money to her dying day.

Perfection, it has been said, is not given to Man; and More would never have claimed to be perfect. But, a frail, ascetic, kindly soul, he was one of the very few who would not swear to what he did not believe. He went to his death for his conscience. The shock his execution caused throughout the Christian world was the measure of his incomparable status.

On 29 January 1935 the Pope declared More to have been a martyr, and beatified; and in May of that year he formally canonized Thomas More as Saint. By a curious irony, 19 May was the anniversary of Anne Boleyn's death.

In studying an historical play it is arguable how far the reader or spectator is helped to understand the plot or background by a study of the historical facts. Certainly the dramatic formula is rather like a 'lightning sketch'. The dramatist relies on a pre-knowledge of the theme and period, rather as an audience of ancient Greeks could be relied on to know the myths on which Euripides, Aeschylus and Sophocles worked. So far as examinations are concerned, the text of the play is what the student will be examined upon – not the More of history. But the fact remains that the play will not yield up its secrets to those who are content to read it casually. Much background information is necessary to supplement the details merely indicated in the text of the play.

Therefore some acquaintance with the primary sources of the history of the period, and More's life in particular, will be valuable – if only for reference. It is only in relatively recent times that a transcript of the trial of More has been available, edited by E. E. Reynolds. More took his defence from the text of the statutes under which he was indicted, in his belief (misguided as it happened) that the letter of the law would be observed, even though the spirit was not. More believed in the Integrity of the Law, the liberty of the individual under that law; that he was defeated is not attributable to his failure to appreciate the law so much as his failure to allow for perjury.

The main sources of More's biography rest on the *Lives* by William Roper, son-in-law and an important character in the play, and also that by Nicholas Harpsfield. The letters of Erasmus are invaluable for an appreciation of More's character, although in fact they refer to the earlier period in More's life. Roper's *Life* was not published until 1626; nearly a century had to elapse before it was considered safe to write about the events that earlier shook a dynasty. Details about the political background can be found in Brewer's *Reign of Henry VIII*.

The historical play

Because the play is set in remote historical times, it is described as 'historical'. Bolt says that 'I took a historical setting in the hope that the distance of years would give me Dutch courage, and enable me to treat my characters in a properly heroic, properly theatrical manner.'

When we speak of a historical play do we refer to the political background of the times in which the play is set and to which it refers? Or is the historical background just chosen by the playwright because it is vivid and colourful, affording opportunity for spectacle and costume? Do the audience who witness an historical play go to the theatre in the hope of seeing a serious examination of the politics of the period? Or do they interpret the play as a kind of allegory on present times, set amid the framework of a historical past? The question is one on which the student will have to make up his own mind: it is impossible to generalize usefully. Historical plays vary enormously, in subject-matter, treatment, depth – some are realistic, some romantic; some are loaded beneath a weighty cargo of archaeological research – others are patently fiction to which a thin veneer of historical authenticity has been added.

The one common denominator of all the plays that could be collected together under the label 'historical' is that they should be actable and that they should 'popularize' history, that is to say they should have a distinct entertainment value, at different levels of intelligence. The aim of the playwright is to present historical episodes with an imaginative vision. The most obvious fact is that history offers colourful and stirring scenes on which the dramatist can fasten his attention. On the other hand, the writer is bound by information already to hand. Distortion of historical characters there may be, but in the main the writer is confined to the popular 'image' of the historical character whom he seeks to portray.

For example, everyone knows that the popular image of Richard III as a Machiavellian villain is largely a myth, ascribable partly to Shakespeare, partly to More as historian and partly to the Tudor need for blackening the usurper's character. As long ago as Horace Walpole, formidable doubts concerning this popular view of Richard had been recorded: for instance, the view that he was a loathsome hunchback had given way to the more accurate view that his unattractive physique was the result of an attack of polio. But for theatrical purposes Richard has been painted a villain, and a villain he remains.

The theatre is not the place for whitewashing Richard. It is not the place for proving that Guy Fawkes was an earnest Presbyterian or that Nell Gwynne was a strict moralist ... the playwright who presents Henry VIII is bound to present him, as the schoolboy said, as a great

widower. William the Silent must not be a chatterbox, nor
Torquemada a humanitarian ... where historic legend exists, he must
respect it at his peril (William Archer).

Legendary and historical characters necessarily remain very
much the creatures of myth that they have always been. A
Napoleon who was not a military genius would be useless for
dramatic purposes. Lloyd Osbourne's play *The Exile* failed in
the theatre because it presented a view of Napoleon that no
one could accept – a Napoleon in decline. It is quite likely that
Napoleon, in later years, *was* in decline. But a theatrical audience is in no mood for such an uncharacteristic view. It wants
to see the Napoleon of tradition. The scholar who is saturated
in the history of the French revolution may know that the
current image of Robespierre as a dreadful tyrant is wholly
mistaken; but no dramatist has been found to take that view.

The aim of historical drama is not to probe truth, cost what it
may in terms of popular acceptance. It follows then that we
must not expect a revaluation of the character of More. Surprisingly Robert Brustein finds *A Man for All Seasons*; 'a faithful
account of More's martyrdom, yet too diffuse to be entirely
successful, yet compared with more vulgarly dramatic bio-
graphies like Anouilh's *Becket* and John Osborne's *Luther* it
shows remarkable accuracy and good taste.'

Brustein has summarized the play as follows:

More, whose conversation according to Erasmus was full of jesting and
fun, has usually been treated on the stage as a madcap: the
Elizabethan play *Sir Thomas More* – erroneously ascribed at one time to
Shakespeare – even has him cracking jokes on the scaffold. Bolt
interprets him more as a melancholy intellectual aristocrat desperately
trying to preserve some corner of private conscience, while preserving
his life at the same time. More is prudent and discreet ('our natural
business lies in escaping') and inclined to protect himself behind
legalistic subterfuges. When asked to swear to the Acts of Succession,
establishing Henry's divorce and his control over the English Church,
he simply maintains silence. Determined not to be a martyr if he can
help it, he could probably defend his strategy with the same aphorism
as Brecht's Galileo – 'Unhappy is the land that needs a hero.' He is
nudged into heroism reluctantly when all the escape routes have been
closed. More's death, the wages of integrity, is for all ages ... but the
moral is for our time.

Voltaire said that 'the history of the great movements of this world is nothing more than the history of crimes'; and when we remember the roll of martyrs in Tudor times we are inclined to agree: the role of the historical playwright is to provide a contemporary scale of reference for ages past. In the true sense of the word history is, as Bolingbroke said, philosophy teaching by examples. This play is essentially a facet of biography: Bolt would agree with Emerson that there is no history without biography. History was the favourite reading of men like Napoleon, Lloyd George and Churchill. And dramatized history was the favourite spectacle of the Elizabethans, who held with Bacon that 'The purpose of history is to make men wise.'

The crux of the play concerns the Oath of Supremacy and it is essential to follow the action closely, and to understand precisely the reasons why More was unable to take the Oath.

Early in 1533 Anne Boleyn was secretly married to Henry VIII. Cranmer, who had succeeded Warham as Archbishop of Canterbury, pronounced the King's marriage with Catherine of Aragon null and void, and the new Queen was crowned in June. More was conspicuous by his absence. His absence provoked the undying enmity of both Anne and Henry.

In 1534 the succession to the Crown was vested in the heirs of this marriage. In the preamble to the Act of Succession the King's marriage with Catherine was expressly stated to be null and void, and his marriage with Anne was stated to be valid. All the King's subjects were required to take this Oath – and Cromwell and Norfolk were appointed Commissioners to ensure that the swearing was carried out. Parliament took the Oath on 30 March 1532. This Oath was regarded as the test of loyalty to Henry, and any who did not take it thus drew attention to their disloyalty – and hence their treason. More then knew himself to be in the gravest danger. Attempts to implicate him in accepting bribes, and in being concerned in the affair of the 'Holy Maid of Kent' (who had prophesied that anyone who supported the Divorce was no longer a Catholic) failed; but the Oath could not be overcome by any legal means. More was now in peril of his life. On 12 April he was required to appear before the commissioners at Lambeth for the purpose of taking the Oath. He refused. All attempts to persuade him to alter his mind failed. On 1 July he was formally brought to trial. On 7 July he was executed. When news of his death was brought to the King, he cast his eye on Anne Boleyn and said, 'You are the cause of this' – and, leaving the table, fell into a fit of melancholy.

So died the man who Dean Swift described as a 'man of the greatest virtue this kingdom has ever produced'.

Act summaries, critical commentary, textual notes and revision questions

Act I

The curtain rises on the Common Man, who stands in front of a large property basket, implying that he is to take several parts. More and Rich are pursuing an argument, and Rich, who is to prove the willing instrument of More's downfall, suggests that every man has his price, a sentiment More deplores. Rich has been attracted by the doctrines of Machiavelli; already he knows who is worth cultivating for his own advantage, and it is evident that he looks to Thomas Cromwell. More tries to persuade him to be a teacher at the new school, but Rich is quite unable to accept this as genuine advice from a man in More's position, and imagines that he is being used as a pawn. We are quickly shown More's family in the characters of Alice his wife and Margaret his daughter. There is also present the great Duke of Norfolk, who would fain see Wolsey brought low. More is then summoned to Cardinal Wolsey's palace at Hampton Court, to which he sets off by river.

Wolsey seeks More's support for the King's divorce but fails to get it.

On his return home, More meets his daughter and Roper, who wants to marry her. He refuses his consent – so long as Roper is a heretic.

The audience is informed that Wolsey has died and that More is the new lord Chancellor. Cromwell, however, appears as the power behind the throne.

The King pays a visit to the garden of Sir Thomas More at Chelsea to talk about his divorce – a chance call, though Cromwell knew of it a week before. Henry refuses to enter the house and leaves in a violent temper when More fails to accede to his wishes.

Before the end of the Act, Cromwell is seen offering profitable positions to Rich in return for his support in bringing about More's downfall, in particular by procuring evidence for a charge of accepting bribes.

every man has his price This maxim was said to have been that of Sir Robert Walpole (1676–1745), generally regarded as the first Prime

Minister. It suggests a popularized version of Machiavellian doctrine. At any rate it is Rich's view. Bolt is not concerned about anachronisms.

bricks-and-mortar Here the language is definitely anachronistic. The phrase used here as a popular metaphor for building was not current until long after Tudor times. But, as has been pointed out above, the playwright is not concerned about accuracy in detail. Like most modern playwrights, he prefers to use anachronisms of language where these will serve his purpose. See also pp.36–7.

Signor Machiavelli The Italian statesman and writer Niccolo di Bernardo dei Machiavelli (1469–1527) was the author of *The Prince*, which was traditionally considered to be inspired by the devil. Machiavelli was popularly regarded as depraved and inhuman, and the Elizabethan dramatists found him a suitable bogey-man for their tragedies. Every villain of stock Renaissance tragedy paid allegiance to Machiavelli, even though none of the playwrights had apparently read him. In England, through the writings of Cardinal Pole, Machiavelli gained a reputation for all that was evil. Every would-be despot liked to think that Machiavelli was his complete guide: an idea that persisted as late as Mussolini. Legend and myth obscured the true facts. Machiavelli was known more by his evil reputation than for his actual writings.

Cambridge Rich had studied at a Cambridge college.

The Cardinal's outer doorman So far Rich has never been able to meet Wolsey. The picture of a throng of hangers-on around a great man of influence is only too familiar.

The Dean of St Paul's This was Dr John Colet, one of the Humanists of the Renaissance. He is traditionally held to have been one of More's teachers. He was a notable scholar, and founded St Paul's school in 1504.

Court of Requests A Court to which even the poorest citizen could go to seek redress; More was Judge of the Court. The Star Chamber was able to deal with powerful nobles; the Court of Requests dealt with complaints against lesser people.

they offer you all sorts of things Bribery was the rule rather than the exception. More as a judge was above reproach, however; he soon justified his reputation for incorruptibility and became famous as the first judge to refuse bribes.

falcon Falconry (or 'hawking') was one of the most popular sports among the aristocracy. A 'cast' was a flight of hawks.

Aristotle (384–322 BC); a Greek philosopher, to whose opinions great authority was attached in Renaissance times.

Act of God A tremendous natural happening away from the normal. The phrase is still used of calamities in nature (e.g. hurricanes and floods) by insurance companies, and in law.

a City Wife A term of abuse, used here to suggest a social climber – a tradesman's wife who wishes to become socially accepted by the nobility.

The Cardinal's Secretary Thomas Cromwell had just been officially appointed Secretary to Wolsey. But he had long been known as the person through whom suitors for Wolsey's favours might best make their applications. He cared nothing at all for his unpopularity with the people; and he was never known to refuse a bribe. In this he was a true Machiavellian – utterly without scruple.

Howard The family name of the Dukes of Norfolk. (Catharine Howard, a member of the same family, became Henry's fifth queen).

A *farrier's* son Cromwell's father was variously said to be a farrier (and therefore an early veterinary surgeon for horses), a brewer, a smith and an armourer. In Tudor times and later, a thriving man often combined several trades. There was much less specialization in life generally. Sir Philip Sidney, the Elizabethan ideal of a gentleman, was courtier, soldier, statesman and man of letters.

The King's business. The Queen's business This was the divorce between Catherine of Aragon and Henry VIII, which in fact is the starting point of the play. Henry's marriage had produced a daughter and six other children who had died at birth or in infancy, and Henry regarded (or affected to regard) this as Nemesis for his disobedience to Old Testament law in marrying his brother's widow. To preserve the Tudor line it was essential that Henry have a male heir; at that time the idea of a female monarch was unthinkable. It was freely prophesied that if a female were to rule, this would be the occasion for a renewal of the Civil Wars of previous reigns, notably the Wars of the Roses. Moves to annul the marriage had begun in 1527, and Wolsey had been engaged in secret overtures; historically, there were many precedents for the divorce of a monarch. Wolsey had hopes of becoming Pope; he did not wish to risk a break with Rome, and he may well have thought that the King would tire of Anne Boleyn if he could procrastinate long enough.

Is there a boat? The River Thames was one of the main highways of communication, East to West.

Are *you* at Richmond? More's house was in Chelsea, so the quickest route to the Cardinal's palace at Richmond was by boat. Richmond was formerly called Sheen: 'resplendent' (there is still a small town called Sheen, near Richmond). When Henry VII rebuilt the Palace after a disastrous fire he called it Richmond after one of his titles.

New Inn One of the Inns of Court. More was a member of this Inn. Barristers were (and still are) enrolled at one of the Inns of Court. New Inn has long since disappeared, however.

Hounslow At the period of the play a country district, suitable for hawking. (Hounslow is today a large suburban town in the county of Middlesex, near London.)

Latin dispatch All documents concerning affairs of state were written in Latin, which was the language used in diplomacy. What we should call the Foreign Secretary was the Latin Secretary.

the Council The King's Council, a policy-making body, composed mainly of nobles during the Tudor period. The Council was gradually changing, however, by including in its membership members of the middle class who could be relied on to support the King against any combination of nobles. The context shows that Wolsey is ignoring the Council, and to that extent More disapproves.

frivel Trifle away time (usually 'frivol').

your scholarship It must not be forgotten that More, though viewed in this play as a statesman, was nevertheless a scholar of the Renaissance, the only rival of Erasmus.

to play in the muck again An indirect reference to the King's affair with Anne Boleyn. Wolsey, as a man of the world, treats this as something to be expected, but More makes it a moral issue.

D'you think two Tudors is sufficient? Wolsey is trying to force More to realize the implications of the matter. If Catherine were to remain Queen the Tudor dynasty would finish. More says he prays that the King may have a son. Wolsey, worldly-wise, is astonished at More's simplicity in these matters: only a miracle could achieve it, and the age of miracles is past.

dispensation The granting of a licence by the Pope to do that which ordinarily is forbidden by the Church.

the Yorkist Wars The Wars of the Roses which had plunged England into civil war. They ended with the elevation of the first Tudor to the throne, Henry VII in 1485. Wolsey is saying that unless Henry VIII has a male heir, the country will again be plunged into the nightmare of civil war.

Councillor There had never been a time in England when there had not been a council, more or less secret, to advice the King, and to act when he was abroad. The Star Chamber was such a council. These Councils were now new, but Henry's use of the Council was an innovation. More was a member of the Council. (See note on 'the Council', above.)

Fisher? Suffolk? John Fisher, Bishop of Rochester, a supporter of Queen Catherine. Because he refused to sanction Anne's marriage and take the oath of succession he was attainted for treason and executed shortly before More's own death. Suffolk was one of the great noblemen, brother-in-law of the King, an opponent of Wolsey. Wolsey wonders which of the three will take over his work. As a matter of historical fact, More succeeded Wolsey as Lord Chancellor, now a purely legal position; Norfolk became Lord President of the Council and Suffolk was Vice-President. Actually, the real power beyond the empty trappings was in the hands of Thomas Cromwell.

licence Students must remember that this is an historical *play*, its basis is fact, with fiction intertwined in its structure. For example, it does not matter whether the necessity of having a licence to ply for hire under a fixed fare schedule on the Thames is historically (i.e. factually) accurate. The point is that the dramatist is drawing a parallel between the way that Cromwell, the dry legalist, treats the common boatman, and More. The playwright treats history metaphorically – not photographically.

You are correctly informed The function of an ambassador was chiefly to act as informant, or, to put it plainly, as a spy, for foreign powers. Chapuys, the agent of the Spanish King (the Emperor Charles V), wishes to sound More on what is happening behind the scenes.

Dominus vobiscum 'The Lord be with you.' Probably used to add a little 'local colour' to the Ambassador's dialogue. Thomas More replies with the current phrase in response – 'and with thy spirit'.

The river looks very black Bolt has told us that he used metaphors for 'the superhuman context of the powers behind events'. The most formidable superhuman metaphor he could think of was the sea, so that throughout the play there are references to the river, currents, tides, navigation and so on.

so long as you're a heretic More was relentless in his pursuit of heretics.

Doctor Luther One of the German leaders of the Reformation. In 1517 Luther had nailed his 95 articles on the door of the Castle Church at Wittenberg. He began by denouncing corruption in the Church and ended by denouncing the Papacy. It might be thought that Henry would have welcomed Luther's doctrines, but he regarded Luther as anathema and the English people were forbidden to read him.

Forgiveness by the florin! Roper has picked up some of Luther's case against the Papacy – dispensations and indulgences. More protests that Luther has been excommunicated; Roper says, 'How can a heretic Church excommunicate?'

Lutherism was very much 'in the air' at the time. Clearly Luther had touched on many a sore spot. Throughout the length and breadth of the land, though Lutherism was unmentionable it had its secret devotees, particularly among the merchant classes.

COMMON MAN (reading) The Common Man uses here a very effective alienation device. He reads, presumably from an imaginary historian writing centuries after the event – presenting an 'objective picture' of the situation; thus the spectator is, as it were, forced to leave the theatre. The information is given that Wolsey has fallen, ironically enough immediately after More's statement that 'There will be no new Chancellors while Wolsey lives.' Incidentally, the date of Wolsey's death should be 1529.

Hampton Court A palace built by Wolsey and presented in 1525 to Henry VIII.

Deptford Trinity House, founded by Henry VIII in 1514; the dockyard was opened the following year – the real beginning of the British Navy.

Great Harry Henry VIII was one of the Tudor monarchs responsible for the growth of the British Navy; this is generally regarded as an example of Henry's foresight and statesmanship. His father Henry VII had ordered the building of the *Royal Harry*, and this is the date generally regarded as the starting point of the modern Navy, with the creation of Trinity House and the Admiralty. It is worth noting that the Navy then consisted of *The Great Harry*, 1200 tons, two ships of 800 tons and seven smaller ships!

it has fifty-six guns by the way The foreign ambassador knows more about the ship than the English politician! More said that it was one of his functions to collect information.

Dominican The Friars were an important part of this religious Foundation. They popularized religion; actually both Henry VIII and Erasmus were opposed to friaries – as being protagonists of obscurantism. It seems strange that More should be made to support them – since he was presumably one of Erasmus's supporters.

rheumatism This is an example of the anachronism, deliberate or otherwise, into which the writer of a historical novel or play can so easily slip. The concept of rheumatism was quite unknown to physicians of More's time, and the word was not used until 1601. Cf. *'kippers'*, and *'magnolias'* (not discovered until 1748). The holly-hock was known in the sixteenth century as the marshmallow.

Plainsong A form of vocal music originating in the Christian Church, of a recitative-like character and sung in unison. It is still in use in Catholic churches.

D'you propose to meet the King … clerk? More often assisted at Mass in Chelsea old church. He is said to have carried the Cross in procession and performed offices usually assigned to the verger. The origin of this scene is to be found in Roper's *Life of More* ('The Mirror of Virtue in Worldly Greatness'). But the occasion was actually in the parish church.

in a cloth of gold Henry's tastes were expensive and showy. Clothes were a 'status symbol', often costing fabulous sums. Later, when More's wife Alice was in poverty, she sold much of the family's rich apparel to provide the means to pay for a servant to attend Sir Thomas in the Tower.

pilot An anachronism (see p.37). The word 'pilot', in the sense of one who guides or steers a boat, was not used until 1693. Similarly what we now know as a rowing-boat was then called a barge, and the word 'dowdy' was first used in 1580, and even then it referred to a woman, not a man.

'There is no end to the making of books … flesh' Henry quotes somewhat sententiously from the Bible (Ecclesiastes xii, 12).

I'm something of a scholar too Tradition has it that Henry was destined to be a great theological scholar, and his father, Henry VII, had him educated for the Church. The utmost pains were bestowed on his education and according to Eramus he was a good scholar. Of course, it was an age when it paid to flatter kings and princes, but everything points to Henry's possessing more than average culture.

the seven sacraments Luther had written a book that seemed perilously near heresy – *De Captivitate Babylonica Ecclesia* – and Henry at once wrote a tract to refute it. In August 1521 Henry's work was sent to Pope Leo, and as a reward the Pope conferred on him the order or title of Fidei Defensor, a title still held by our monarchs (this is what the abbreviation FID DEF, or FD on our coins stands for). In 1534 Cranmer, Norfolk and Cromwell met to examine More; they charged him with provoking Henry to set forth his assertion of the seven sacraments in order to maintain the Pope's authority, thus putting a sword in the Pope's hands against Henry ('Your father had a hand in that; eh, Thomas?') More denied the charge and said that one day the Pope might use the book against Henry.

it was never merry in England while we had Cardinals These words are here put into the mouth of Henry, but they were actually spoken by the Duke of Suffolk on the day when Campeggio was expected to give his decision on the divorce. Instead, he adjourned the case because of the vacation at the Pope's court. This was so obviously a flimsy excuse that the Duke of Suffolk, enraged, uttered the words quoted. From that moment (23 July 1529) Wolsey's fate was sealed.

Dogget's Bank. Tilbury Roads Tilbury is now known for its docks. A road is a sheltered stretch of water near the shore where vessels may safely harbour. Dogget's Bank is an imaginary place.

wick i.e. flame.

the Great Seal The symbol of the office of Lord Chancellor.

Leviticus. Deuteronomy The law of Moses, which nobody could doubt was the law of God. Though Deuteronomy (xxv,5) does not agree with Leviticus and approves of the marriage of a widow with her husband's brother.

Strictly speaking according to canon law the Catholic Church did not allow divorce, but there were 'impediments to marriage', and if impediments existed then a marriage was null and void. An ecclesiastical court might pronounce a marriage even of many years standing as invalid and such declarations were far from uncommon. Henry's sister was allowed to have her marriage to the Duke of Suffolk put aside, for instance. Henry's request was ordinary enough. But diplomatic considerations entered. And these diplomatic considerations proved insuperable in the Pope's eyes.

the Holy See i.e. the office of Pope.

Princes of the *Church* i.e. in opposition to the *true* Prince.

the Bishop of Rome with the Emperor Pope Clement V with Charles V of Spain. The Pope was in the power of the Spanish King.

nice Particular. (For once a word in its old meaning.)

Lady Anne i.e. Anne Boleyn.

soupçon Little bit.

Joshua's trumpet A reference to the Biblical story of how the walls of Jericho were blown down (Joshua, vi,20).

in the King's party i.e. one of those who supported the King in the divorce and were prepared to make a break with Rome. More was not.

With your views on Church Reformation Roper had once been a sort of Lutheran on the question of reforms within the Church. The great majority of ordinary folk had no desire to change – they grumbled but did nothing. Roper denounced abuses within the Church ('the money-changers in the temple'); probably he cared nothing for justification by faith and predestination – the philosophical basis of Lutherism – but he denounced the abuses of an ignorant clergy who had no notions of their holy vocation and brought their Church into disrepute.

the money-changers . . . scourged from thence A reference to the occasion when Jesus overthrew the tables of the money-changers in the temple, Matthew, xxi,12, Mark, xi,15, John, ii,13–16.

Sophistication The use of specious arguments deliberately to mislead; the cant of philosophers.

the golden calf See Exodus, xxxii.

He sounds like Moloch The God of the Ammonites, who demanded as a sacrifice that which was held most dear, e.g. a son or a daughter. See Kings, xxiii,10, and Milton, *Paradise Lost*, 1,392–7.

A publican Another anachronism: the word has come to bear the meaning of 'a licensed victualler who keeps an ale-house, inn or tavern', but this meaning only came about after the Excise Act of 1728.

Secretary to the Council Each office is in an ascending order of importance. It was Rich who said, 'Every man has his price.'

Revision questions on Act I

1 'More loved God. But he loved the World also.' Give examples from Act I of More's attitude towards (*a*) God, (*b*) the World.

2 What evidence in Act I do you find that More was an intellectual leader?

3 'More enjoyed the company of the king.' Show examples from the text that support this view.

4 Summarize the arguments put forward by Henry for his divorce.

5 Would you agree that More is timid? Give your reasons.

6 'The dialogue adapts itself naturally to the eminent and royal, and also to lesser people.' How far does the text bear this out in Act I?

Act II

Between the two Acts, events have gone forward two years (from early in 1530 to the middle of May 1532).

Roper, now Margaret's husband, has ceased to be a heretic – not in order to win a wife but because he resents the Act of Supremacy. The Imperial Ambassador (Chapuys) comes to seek More's help on behalf of Queen Catherine. He has, he says, made a tour of the North Country and reports that the people are ready to resist, but we hear from Norfolk that 'one of Secretary Cromwell's agents made the tour with him'! We are told that Convocation (see note p.23) has 'knuckled under' (and is to pay a fine of £100,000) and that the English connection with Rome has been severed. More takes off his chain, as a symbol that he resigns his office. He thinks that he will be left alone, if he governs his tongue, and assumes that he cannot be proceeded against since he has made no statement. 'When they find I'm silent they'll ask nothing better than to leave me silent; you'll see.' More's household is reduced and in poorer circumstances.

In the next episode Cromwell draws the net closer and brings up the cup incident again (see end of Act I), calling the woman who gave the cup to More to testify, but Norfolk ridicules and disproves any suggestion that More was bribed; Cromwell tells him, however, that the King wishes him to be active in the matter, and he realizes that 'Sir Thomas is going to be a slippery fish, Richard; we need a net with a finer mesh'.

The Steward (the Common Man) is now Steward to the successful Rich. More's house is drab and chilly, and his family are in a poor way. He is, however, still acting very correctly; for example when there is another approach from the Spanish Ambassador.

Sir Thomas is sent for by Cromwell 'to answer certain charges' – later defined as 'some ambiguities of behaviour'. (A parallel episode to the one in Act I where Wolsey sent for him.) Cromwell first vaguely offers to reward him if he submits, then cross-examines him. But he withstands Cromwell intelligently; nothing can be proved against him, and he is allowed to go home. But now it is evident that More is out of favour – he cannot get a boatman to row him home. Norfolk appears on the waterfront and tells him that he is behaving like a fool and that he is a dangerous man to know.

A new Act is passed (or driven) through Parliament, by which an oath is to be administered on penalty of treason. More wants to get home and study the wording. Then the Common Man sets a new scene and More has been a year in prison and looks much older. He is about to be examined yet again, this time by Cromwell, Norfolk and Archbishop Cranmer – 'the Seventh Commission to enquire into the case of Sir Thomas More'. More recognizes the offspring of Queen Anne as heirs to the throne, but will not take the Oath. Cromwell vindictively orders him to be left without books in his cell.

He is anxious to obtain More's submission, for if he brings about More's death he may be sowing the seeds of his own. He therefore arranges for More's family and Roper to plead with him. But they fail to move him, and indeed they give him an opportunity to plot their flight from the country. It is obvious that More realizes that to heed their words would have been his last chance.

More is tried. Rich gives perjured evidence; More admits that he is 'a dead man'. Norfolk reads the sentence.

And the Common Man performs his last office – as the executioner of More.

Convocation An assembly of the Church whose absolute submission Henry required. In May 1532 he appointed a commission of thirty-two learned men, including laymen, who would revise the existing canon law. Thus intimidated, the clergy surrendered their power; Henry obtained his object and was absolute master. The following day Sir Thomas More resigned his office of Lord Chancellor. In the words of Chapuys, the Church had less authority over its priests than the shoemakers had over their craft. As Roper puts it, 'The Church is already a wing of the Palace.'

its 'Supreme Head' Henry had ordered the clergy to acknowledge him, not the Pope, as Supreme Head of the Church.

Signor Chapuys Chapuys is an agent of the Spanish, not the Italian, monarch, and the proper word would therefore be Señor.

What do you require of _me_? More has grown accustomed to associate praise with ulterior motives.

the English Socrates Socrates was another Greek philosopher to whose opinions great authority was attached (cf. Aristotle, note p.15). More had been called 'the English Socrates' by Erasmus. His reference to hemlock recalls the fact that when condemned to death Socrates committed suicide by drinking hemlock – More has no taste for martyrdom.

Cheapside A market district in the City of London (originally from Anglo-Saxon 'ceap', barter or purchase). Incidentally, it was first called Cheapside in 1510.

Dominus...excellencis! God be with you, my children! And with thy spirit, your excellency! Cf. note p.18.

I have just returned...Northumberland Chapuys is reporting the state of unrest that was later to result in the Pilgrimage of Grace (1536), provoked by the Dissolution of the Monasteries. As a matter of historical fact, Chapuys was quite frequently the means of stirring up trouble on behalf of Charles V. Spanish intervention was always a possibility that Henry had to reckon with, and that was the real reason for his founding the Navy, so as to repel a possible invader.

Convocation's knuckled under The Church raised £100,000, which was in effect a fine, and Convocation had difficulty in raising the money. On 16 May the Archbishop delivered to the King the formal document known as 'The Submission of the Clergy'. This was the tacit acknowledgement that the King was ruler of the Church, whereupon More surrendered the Chancellorship.

Bishop Fisher See note p.17.

puts his hand to his chain Representing his office.

Our King, Norfolk, has declared war on the Pope The practical effect of all this was that the King had abandoned his position as a Catholic monarch. Norfolk does not dispute that 'we're at war with the Pope'.

the Border i.e. between Scotland and England. The 'Old Alliance' is that between Scotland and France.

The Dago A term of contempt for a Spaniard, here referring to Chapuys, the Imperial Ambassador.

It's good to know...patriotism Patriotism in the modern sense was a concept unknown to the early Tudors. It is an Elizabethan notion. The first use of the word was in 1596.

I'll write a bit More in fact spent much of his new-found leisure in writing. As a result he was charged by his enemies to be receiving money from Church funds for writing tracts supporting Popery, to which he replied, 'Men were wont to suspect people of heresy. Now the new suspects are those suspected of the Catholic Faith.' In fact, More turned down all offers of money from friends who realized his dire poverty.

acrobat The first use of the word in English was not until 1825. Here Bolt deliberately uses a word that he knows is an anachronism, because it has the right slant of meaning for his audience.

You'd dance him . . . block Many executions took place in the Tower in the time of Henry VIII. The reference to David is to 2 Samuel, vi, 1–16.

even stevens Rhyming slang, a form of vulgar popular speech used by cockneys (e.g. 'Charley Prescott' for 'waistcoat'), plain to fellow cockneys, while it leaves others ignorant and mystified.

Cato A Roman judge (234–149 BC) renowned for his absolute incorruptibility: a simple man of brusque manners and blunt speech, but strict in justice.

You had a cup with you See Act I, pp.4–9. This effort to fasten bribes on More retrospectively failed. The historical fact is that a suitor called Vaughan sent his wife to present More with a cup. More was charged with the offence before the Council, but was able to prove his innocence. Bolt dramatizes this by foreshortening the scene.

I begin to need a steward, certainly The Common Man (Steward) significantly changes his allegiance as the men in power requiring stewards change.

incognito Are we to suppose that so cunning an agent was not aware that he was being watched? In any event Norfolk had said that the 'Dago' (Chapuys) was always under the surveillance of one of Cromwell's agents.
    The first use of the word 'incognito' was not until 1610. Compare the metaphors from horse-racing, which was not a popular Tudor pastime.

pragmatist Pragmatism – a word not used until 1902 – is the doctrine that a thing is to be judged by its practical consequences; hence More likens the pragmatist Cromwell to 'the merest plumber'.

That's a nice gown At the beginning of Act I (p.4) Rich told More that he wanted 'some decent clothes'. More's remark is ironical.

Some ambiguities . . . clarify This is the language of the twentieth-century Civil Service. Bolt is showing Cromwell as a master of George Orwell's 'double-think'. The language was known in Tudor times even if the linguistic expression for it was not.

the so-called 'Holy Maid of Kent' Elizabeth Barton, an epileptic said to have been cured by the Virgin Mary, prophesied in trances, and amongst those who had listened to her were Fisher and More – even Wolsey and the King himself had listened to her 'revelations'. Ultimately she was brought to the Star Chamber, for she had foretold dire penalties for those who aided and abetted the Royal divorce.

Charge? More calls the word in question since Cromwell had said his clarification of 'some ambiguities of behaviour' hardly amounted to 'charges'.

the Sermon on the Mount The Beatitudes (Matthew v, 1–12). More says that the nobility of England are more interested in breeding dogs than in the Sermon on the Mount!

Thomas Aquinas A renowned philosopher and theologian (1225–74), author of the *Summa Theologia*, the most perfect expression of Catholic orthodoxy.

wittily It would appear that the word is used with the sixteenth-century meaning from 'wit', with wisdom, judgement.

nearer the knuckle Less respectable.

Act of Succession This Act of 1534 was thoroughgoing and comprehensive. Mere speaking against the Act was made an offence.

the Lieutenant i.e. of the Tower.

The Attorney-General for Wales Wales was not united with England until 1536, hence the office was distinct from that of the English Attorney-General. The red dragon is a traditional emblem of Wales.

some gentler way Cromwell now tries to weaken More's resolution by persuasion by his family.

the Hall of Westminster From the very earliest days the Great Hall of the Palace of Westminster was used as a court of law, especially for important State trials.

forthink Be sorry for.

wit Good sense.

betoken Mean.

construe Explain.

Sir Richard Southwell and Master Palmer ... what was said This is historically correct.

it profits a man nothing ... the whole world See Matthew, xvi, 26, Mark viii, 36.

The case rests This is an Americanism, never heard in English courts.

Magna Carta The foundation of the liberties of Englishmen, or at least of English barons, sealed by King John in 1215, and confirmed over thirty times by later monarchs. It begins by promising the immunity of the Church; this is still a part of the monarch's Coronation Oath.

easel and gall Presumably a reference to the vinegar and gall that Christ was given to drink just before he was crucified (Matthew, xxvii, 34).

Revision questions on Act II

1 Summarize the course of the quarrel between King Henry and More in Act II.

2 Trace the growing importance of Cromwell in the play after the death of Wolsey.

3 Describe the course of events at the trial of More in the Hall of Westminster.

4 At the end of Act I Rich declares that More 'doesn't know how to be frightened', but Cromwell doubts it. Show which of the two proves right in Act II.

5 'More's family life meant much to him.' What evidence is there in Act II to support this view?

6 'The play lacks variety.' How far is this criticism justified, especially in Act II?

Plot and structure

Bolt says that he tried for a story rather than a plot. The play is loosely thrown into the form of what used to be called the Chronicle play. From time to time the theatre throws up a recrudescence of this episodic form, with results mostly indifferent. Plays like Anouilh's *L'Alouette* (Joan of Arc) and T. S. Eliot's *Murder in the Cathedral* (Becket), Albert Camus's *Caligula*, Norman Ginsburg's *First Gentleman* (George IV), John Drinkwater's *Abraham Lincoln* and Bernard Shaw's *Saint Joan* are all examples of a *genre* that has from time to time given us outstanding works.

As it happened, in the 1960s there was quite a spate of historical dramas in the London theatre; Terence Rattigan's *Ross* (Lawrence of Arabia) and John Osborne's *Luther* had shown that there was always an audience for the new interpretation of historical figures.

What has to be remembered is that a historical play is not to be regarded as a theatrical presentation of history. In other words the dramatist does not set up in rivalry with the historian. His purpose is not historical but a psychological interpretation.

Nor must objective accuracy in the presentation of events be expected. The overriding consideration must always be the dramatic conception. The dramatist is not concerned with the niceties of historical fact but rather with the broad sweep of events. To this end he may ignore the calendar; he may find it necessary to transpose events, to telescope them, to alter dates so as to bring them within some sort of dramatic unity.

In *A Man for All Seasons* Robert Bolt has allowed himself the licence that is the latitude of the creator. He is not concerned with mere accuracy: he is not an archaeologist of Tudor events; the student must not go to the play expecting to see a dramatic transcription of the latest historical research.

The best known historical play is probably Shakespeare's *Henry V*, and it will be a useful scholastic exercise to compare the structure of *Henry V* with Bolt's play. In both plays a number of short episodes are linked together, these episodes are in the main founded on historical fact, but in order to secure variety some latitude is allowed so that the play illustrates varied aspects of the 'hero'. It is obvious that no play could present the full biographical facts, so that the dramatist is forced to select and simplify – and to that extent every historical play must be a distortion of precise history.

Nevertheless the principles of construction are broadly the same. In the place of Shakespeare's Chorus, Bolt presses into service The Common Man, about whom we shall have more to say presently. On the occasion of the original first performance in London, on 1 July 1960, the programme carried a note by the playwright.

The action of this play ends in 1535, but the play was written in 1960; and if in production one date must obscure the other it is 1960 which I would clearly indicate to occupy the stage. The *life* of a man like More offers a number of caps which, in this or any other century, we may try on for size.

Bolt's note gives us a clue to the kind of play *A Man for All Seasons* is. Using Sir Thomas More as a titular symbol, the play is concerned with an eternal theme: how far along the road of what is called expediency (Shakespeare in *King John* called it commodity) a man may go before he is brought to a halt; to the point where something that we can call conscience steps in and says 'Thus far, and no farther:' More did not want to be a martyr; for a time he relied on all the quibbles of legality, he took refuge in every trick in the lawyer's book; but in the last analysis he saw his position quite clearly. The play is really a study of passive resistance against authoritarianism. It is a dilemma that is always with us – sometimes in the form of high comedy, sometimes profound tragedy.

As in Shaw's *Saint Joan*, the dramatist has been scrupulously fair; apart from Henry VIII, there are no real villains in this piece. (As Shaw said, 'A villain in a play can be nothing better than a *diabolus ex machina* ... possibly a more exciting expedient than a *deus ex machina*, but both equally mechanical, and therefore interesting only as a mechanism.')

The play begins at the moment when More is apparently firmly entrenched as Master of Requests, a form of judgeship; he is not yet Lord Chancellor and Wolsey is still in the ascendant. But already two men appear who will play a great part in the later scenes of the drama – Richard Rich, who is so unimportant that More's Steward can afford to dismiss him as a mere nonentity. Later he is to be the Solicitor-General who perjures himself to secure More's conviction; the other man is Thomas Cromwell – who is at first mentioned only as a student of Machiavelli.

As has been indicated, the play is enacted through a series of episodes, played continuously; between them the changes of scene are bridged by the device of the appearance of the Common Man who who plays a number of small parts of minor importance that link together these successive episodes. The importance of this stage character will be discussed in detail (in the section on *Characters*). Suffice it here to say that he is something of a 'Brechtian' Chorus who plays all the lower-class characters, a greedy opportunist who takes every chance to point out that, 'It isn't difficult to keep alive – just don't make any trouble.' This character is clearly modelled on the Story teller in Bertolt Brecht's *Caucasian Chalk Circle*, perhaps he owes something as well to the ubiquitous Narrator in radio plays, bearing in mind that Bolt served an apprenticeship as BBC script-writer and dramatic producer.

The play has a timeless and universal relevance; though times changes, men remain the same; psychological motives remain constant. There are despots today, as there were in 1535; then, as now, there were men who were prepared to swear to anything.

The printed play is divided into two acts. But for the purposes of studying the play, it will be convenient to split the text of each act into a number of smaller scenes or episodes, bearing in mind that the action runs continuously without pause, save for the incursion, at intervals, of the Common Man – who steps on to the stage, partly to stage-manage the properties, and partly to comment on the action: a combination of epic and dramatic methods. When Garrick produced Shakespeare's *Henry V*, he chose to play the role of Prologue – and it may be that many spectators will think the Common Man is an equally attractive acting role.

The play is not concerned with More's earlier life; for example, no one would ever suspect that More was one of the leaders of the humanist movement in England; or that he was a satirist whose *Utopia* is one of the world's important literary documents; or that he was the scourge of heretics. The play is almost exclusively concerned with More as an honourable man with an inconvenient conscience, one who hopes, by passive resistance, to escape his fate. But he cannot escape his conscience, and his doom is inevitable.

Theme and style

Theme

William Archer, one of the greatest of English dramatic critics, once said that the first step towards writing a play was to choose a theme. But he admitted that such a simple statement required careful examination before its full import was grasped.

The themes of Bolt's play may conveniently be said to be integrity and passive resistance. The dramatist himself has written, 'It is not easy to know what a play is about until it is finished, and by then what it is "about" is incorporated in it irreversibly and is no more to be separated from the work as a whole than the shape of a statue is to be separated from the marble.'

This play most certainly did not arise through a conscious process of selection, followed by the choice of the More story as an illustration. The dramatist did not say, 'I will now write a play about passive resistance – a play of protest about the necessity of not submitting to the establishment – and I will take Henry VIII and Anne Boleyn as an illustration.'

Indeed Bolt is not a dramatist of protest in the ordinary meaning of the phrase at all; but it is true that we are all more or less 'political animals' nowadays. Detachment from the political scene is no longer possible, since modern weapons overshadow life everywhere. 'The problem facing Neville Harrison, Thomas More and Urbain Grandier [the heroes of three plays considered by the critic Harold Hobson] is essentially the same problem. They are at grips with forces immeasurably greater than themselves. They exist in the twentieth century and in the sixteenth century – the impossibility of leading private lives.' The ivory tower is no longer a permissible retreat.

This view of the theme is what first attracted the dramatist. More was a famous man, who would generally be thought of as belonging to the privileged classes. Even so, he felt that, without a belief in 'a power above ourselves' – a belief in the scruples of conscience – life is valueless. He knew that one cannot whittle away conscience. Far from being a martyr, he was timid.

But in the last resort, he could face up to the most monstrous tyranny rather than submit to blasphemy. And the taking of an oath, knowing it to be blasphemy, was exactly that.

More was a very orthodox Catholic and for him an oath was something perfectly specific. It was an invitation to God, . . . the consequence of perjury was damnation. . . . So for More the issue was simple (though remembering the outcome it can hardly have been easy). *Robert Bolt's Preface to the printed play.*

The essential conflict in the play lies between the powers that represent giving way to blasphemy, and More's personal integrity – his belief in the inviolability of an oath. It is symbolical of the conflict doomed to take place whenever vested authority is challenged by the pure in heart. But the play is not a mere dramatic illustration of a textbook moral. The essence of the play is in the character of Thomas More. Indeed, without that character, the theme itself would be arid and dry. Independent of character, passive resistance would be a very uninteresting tussle indeed.

To many readers of the play and spectators in the audience, it may seem strange that More was so adamant about what may seem a mere interpretation of religious dogma. The play may seem to be a revival of 'battles long ago', but to take this view would be to minimize the importance of the theme. More was concerned with human liberty, with conscience and with honour.

It may be that on a very technical point the entire reality of a doctrine may exist. In one sense it may seem to us, centuries afterwards, that the tussle between Henry VIII and the Church of Rome was an academic exercise, and may not have seemed worth the sacrifice of a single life. But deeper reflection will show that the struggle was a classic pattern of the struggle between forces of crucial importance. More defended the paramount authority of the collective Church against individual judgement. This controversy in fact had decisive effects on the national heritage.

What many present-day students cannot understand is the respect that More had for Henry VIII as King. To understand this properly, we must rid ourselves of the popular image of Henry.

More was a pre-Reformation Roman Catholic. That is, he believed mankind should be subject to a hierarchy. The very word is suspect nowadays: but, to More, Christian life was unthinkable without a system of hierarchy – the divine law of subordination and mutual dependence of the different ranks of created beings, human and angelic.

The order in heaven was reproduced on earth; so to be a true subject of the King was the proper duty of a Catholic citizen. Despite the efforts of latter day critics to identify More with the theories he preached satirically in *Utopia*, he was in no sense a political revolutionary. His whole attitude was one of compliance with the law.

Style

So far as style is concerned, the play is not particularly noteworthy. There is no great regard for words, or any unusual technique in their handling. Unlike Harold Pinter, Bolt does not show any specific interest in using words as a theatrical vehicle. The vocabulary is adequate, but not in itself strikingly impressive. There are no speeches that the student feels impelled to learn by rote for the sake of their beauty. Even in the speeches of More there is nothing that is specifically striking. When the role was first played by Paul Scofield in London, it was noteworthy because he rarely raised his voice, and only in the final trial scene did he rely on vocal effect. Obviously the play is written with a view to ensemble playing. This is another point of technique that Bolt probably learned from Brecht. Solo performance, *prima donna* acting is frowned upon; the team-effect is what matters.

The visual appearance and a thumb-nail sketch of each character is given in Bolt's notes on 'people in the Play'; but Bolt does not copy the technique of Bernard Shaw and Barrie and incorporate his characters' appearance in the stage directions.

There is nothing specifically individual or characteristic that can be taken as marking Bolt's style. In a play by Wilde or Coward or Maugham, the lines sparkle and scintillate so that the authorship is instantly obvious. Often indeed in the works of these playwrights epigrams tend to come independently of the character supposed to be speaking them. The characters are in fact but the mouthpiece of the author.

The attraction of Bolt's play lies more in its subject-matter than in the form of its presentation. There are no long set speeches, no soliloquies (no long involved arguments like the Inquisitor's in Shaw's *Saint Joan*). But that is not Bolt's way. His dialogue is very much in the present-day tradition of English writing: the characters reveal their true nature in what they say – and the speech, though in simple, often quiet and understated prose, is entirely revealing. See, for example, how at the beginning of the play Bolt exposes the real characters of More, his Steward and Rich – and their feelings about one another (Act I, pp.2–5). We have seen the Steward sampling More's jug of wine; then More enters:

MORE: The wine please, Matthew?
STEWARD: It's there, Sir Thomas.
MORE (*looking into the jug*): Is it good?
STEWARD: Bless you, sir! I don't know.
MORE (*mildly*): Bless you too, Matthew.

Shortly afterwards, the Steward, when announcing 'Master Richard Rich', puts into his voice all the contempt of a servant who does not consider a visitor to be the social equal of his employer. When Rich says, 'Good evening, Matthew', the Steward merely answers, 'Evening, sir'. Later (p.4), when More offers Rich a silver cup, and Rich accepts it, Bolt writes the following dialogue for them:

MORE: You'll sell it, won't you?
RICH: Yes, I think so. Yes, I will.
MORE: And buy, what?
RICH (*sudden ferocity*): Some decent clothes!
MORE (*with sympathy*): Ah.
RICH: I want a gown like yours.
MORE: You'll get several gowns for that I should think. It was sent to me a little while ago by some woman. Now she's put a lawsuit into the Court of Requests. It's a bribe, Richard.
RICH: Oh. . . (*Chagrined.*) So you give it away of course.
MORE: Yes!
RICH: To me?
MORE: Well, I'm not going to keep it, and you need it. Of course – if you feel it's contaminated . . .
RICH: No no. I'll risk it. (*Both smile*).

And Bolt's deceptively simple prose can be extremely moving, as in More's last words to his daughter: 'Have patience and trouble not thyself. Death comes for us all; even at our birth (. . .) – even at our birth, death does but stand aside a little. It is the law of nature, and the will of God. You have long known the secrets of my heart. (Act II, p.98).

The scenes fade into one another rapidly – held together by the Common Man, who appears, as it were, to bridge the gap. Indeed, he often seems to be employed as a device to lower the temperature rather than to raise it.

When writing his plays, Robert Bolt always uses a small model theatre stage, which he has specially made, to help him while plotting the action. And it can be seen that he always has the stage picture clearly before him. Every theatrical effect has been cleverly thought out; in *A Man for All Seasons* the stage effects are always part of the creation and play a large part in the play's success (e.g. the lighting effects throughout).

Historical faithfulness is not the main concern in this play. Faithfulness to the past, in the sense of naturalism and regard for authenticity, is not of the first importance. It might be thought that faithfulness to the past would be the primary consideration of every historical dramatist, but this is not so.

Perhaps it will be helpful to quote in this connection a comment of Goethe, himself a foremost practitioner of the art of historical plays, such as *Egmont* and *Goetz von Berlichingen*. Goethe is dealing with the question of dialogue in Manzoni's historical tragedy *Adelchi*.

I pronounce in Manzoni's defence what may seem to be a paradox. Whenever we evoke in the past, in order to recite it after our own fashion to a contemporary audience, we translate the antique event. To all ancient conditions one lends a modern spirit, for only through modern ears can we hear and understand old things.

In other words a modern audience must have a historical theme served in the atmosphere and outlook of modern times. Mere deference to historical accuracy is not enough. For example, it does not help the audience one iota if the actual historical background is presented in all its archaeological *minutiae*. The material has to be recast so that attitudes and ideas become clear to people trained in a later way of expression and understanding. It is sufficient if the author succeeds in introducing nothing that is inconsistent with the age and its manners. The spirit is more important than the letter.

Bolt disregards anachronisms (i.e. historical inaccuracies) of style and subject-matter. But that is only in order to enable him to communicate more freely with modern audiences. He scorns the time-honoured device of historical playwrights – a private language meant to indicate remoteness of time; there are no *gadzooks, zounds,* 'by my halidom', and similar resurrections of times gone by. (cf. p.29, 'it is 1960 which I would clearly indicate to occupy the stage.') Shakespeare was full of anachronisms because he just did not bother about them, but Bolt admits them deliberately. Until fairly recent years anachronism was always avoided on the stage, and correctness of detail in local colour was insisted upon. Bolt's attitude is thus in many respects a throwback to older theatrical practice. He brings into service the language of all times, according to the mood of the moment, if he feels he wants a sixteenth-century flavour or a smack of 1960. By the side of 'forthink', 'wit' and 'nice' in their old senses, 'easel and gall', one is startled by the everyday language of TV – 'some decent clothes', 'police work', 'like a bat in a Sunday School' etc., and even an Americanism not familiar in English: 'the case rests'. At other times sixteenth-century words are used in their modern sense (e.g. 'publican' and 'pilot') and other later additions over the centuries are introduced, e.g. 'acrobat'.

There are no fictitious or imaginary characters in this play. Unlike many other dramatists, Bolt found all the material he needed in the authentic characters, without the intrusion of specially invented ones. From which it is but a step to the use of passages actually uttered by More in real life. 'My concern was to match these as best I could so that the theft should not be too obvious,' says Bolt in his Preface.

The characters

Sir Thomas More

You are honest. What's more to the purpose, you're known to be honest.

The outstanding character in the play is, of course, Sir Thomas More himself. The dramatist has seen him as a man in his late forties; though in fact the play will not stand up to exact chronological tests. The action starts at a point when the end is inevitable. Right at the beginning we are introduced to young Rich who later in the play will turn out to be a double-dyed traitor to More. And with the incident of the goblet – a gift from one of More's litigants, which More presents to Rich – the audience is given a subtle foretaste of Rich's treacherous nature.

More is essentially a social man with a real sense of the importance of family life. Bolt has himself referred to More's 'splendid social adjustment'. More was not a rebel, one of civilization's discontents: on the contrary, he was almost a complete conformist. Bolt has likened him to the hero of Albert Camus's *La Chute* – a man 'almost indecently successful'.

The play is entirely concerned with the reversal in More's fortunes. We are not shown the steps by which More ascended to his leading position in the state. When the curtain rises he is already a renowned figure, and Rich appears as a young man 'on the make' who has singled out More precisely because he is a leading counsellor of the King, a man who seems to have 'the golden touch' – a man who has effortlessly 'made the grade'.

Yet nowhere is More made to appear conscious of his own rank. He is far more concerned with his family; as he says,

I was commanded into office. It was inflicted on me – Can't you believe that?

There is no sense of self-importance; yet the part of More is not an exercise in self-humiliation. He is essentially the soul of the play – but he scorns heroics. He is as far removed from the operatic type of character as possible. He does not set out to be a martyr; the author is at some pains to reveal his weaknesses rather than his symbolical strength. He is pictured as pale, middle-sized with spindly legs, not robust. He has no stereotyped façade to present to the public. He knows the world, but cynicism is not his stock in trade. Although his mind is cast in a witty mould he has not the Falstaffian gift of making himself a butt of others' wit.

Early in the play he advises Rich on the value of a quiet life, but that ambitious self-seeker can only think that More is joking, when in fact he has never been more serious. Many are the aspects of More that are not stressed: his great scholarship and his religious asceticism are only touched on in the lightest of terms. One would never realize, for example, that this More is the author of *Utopia*.

He is pictured as devout, in an age when religion was taken very seriously. Yet a careful observer of people, such as Wolsey, realized from the first that it is precisely this 'moral squint' that distinguishes More from a thousand other lawyers and self-seekers. It is Wolsey who says, 'With just a little common sense you could have been a statesman.'

More is shown in contact with many different characters – with Cromwell, with Rich, with Henry, with Norfolk, with Chapuys – but always we feel that he is an individual character. Bolt has himself stated in his Shavian-type Preface,

He was respectably not nobly born, in . . . the progressive class of the epoch . . . A visitors' book at his house in Chelsea would have looked like a Sixteenth Century *Who's Who*: Holbein, Erasmus, Colet, everybody. He corresponded with the greatest minds in Europe as the representative and acknowledged champion of the New Learning in England . . . He adored and was adored by his own large family. He parted with more than most men when he parted with his life, for he accepted and enjoyed his social context.

Above all he reposed a great trust in the workings of the Law – and in this respect he was a traditional Englishman; he felt that he could rely on the Law.

More's trust in the law was his trust in his society; his desperate sheltering beneath the forms of the law was his determination to remain within the shelter of society. Cromwell's contemptuous shattering of the forms of law by an unconcealed act of perjury showed how fragile for any individual is that shelter. Legal or illegal had no further meaning.

More is not depicted as a religious zealot; in this respect Bolt has minimized the evidence. A characteristic that has impressed many students of More, his zeal against heretics, is here confined to a stern treatment of his son-in-law William Roper, who at the beginning of the play is a passionate Lutheran but shifts his position as the play develops.

The play revolves around two poles of action: the events that led up to the martyrdom, and the family circle. It is in keeping with what the historians have told us, that he was a plain man, completely without that exhibitionism and egotism that is too often the hallmark of the 'self-made' man. In an age that was notorious for its costly apparel, More's own clothing was modest, the only sign of his status being a gold chain said to be a Lancastrian badge instituted by Henry IV, and symbolic of his office as Chancellor of the Duchy of Lancaster. We have it on the authority of Erasmus that he wore no other ornaments, no silks, no velvets. The one genuinely contemporary portrait of More painted by a contemporary was owned by Henry VIII and thrown out of the window by Anne Boleyn.

His family circle was his real life, including his house and his garden. In the play this family circle is represented by his daughter Margaret and his wife Alice. Even in his own family circle there were seemingly those who wondered why More made such a fuss of the oath-taking. Alice, his wife, thought so; she would have agreed with Henry Pattesen, the court-jester, who wondered why Sir Thomas More would not bring himself to take the oath, since the court-jester had found no difficulty! Alice puts her finger on the real issue when she says in response to More's direct question, 'What would you *want* me to do?' – 'Be ruled! If you won't rule him [Henry VIII], be ruled.' To which More replies, 'There's a little ... little area where I must rule myself.' He would not surrender his conscience. Alice beseeches him to be circumspect – to stay friends with the King, and More replies, 'Whatever can be done by smiling, you may rely on me to do.'

His family circle never seemed to have understood the man. Neither Roper who regards him as too sophisticated, nor Alice who regards him as too headstrong, has the faintest conception of the real More. Roper sees in More a sophisticated man. To which More replies that it is not sophistication, but sheer simplicity. 'The law ... I know what's legal not what's right. And I'll stick to what's legal.' Roper maintains that as a result More would give the Devil himself the benefit of the law (in contrast to himself, who would cut down every law in England to get at the Devil). To the argument that man must give the Devil the benefit of the law, if only for the safety the law will provide, Roper says that he had long suspected it. 'This is the golden calf; the law's your god.' But More is unshaken: 'Whoever hunts for me . . . will find me hiding in the thickets of the law! And I'll hide my daughter with me!' Summing up his position, More tries to reassure his family. 'I have not disobeyed my sovereign. I truly believe no man in England is safer than myself.' When Alice asks, 'Why then does Cromwell collect information about you?' he retorts, 'I'm a prominent figure. Someone somewhere's collecting information about Cromwell.' Such is the position at the fall of the curtain in Act I. In Act II, the time has come when More is forced to abandon all dependence on legality and to rely on first principles.

In the second act, the threads of the action laid down in the first act are drawn tightly – escape is impossible. Nothing short of a *deus ex machina* will enable More to extricate himself, and the dramatist no less than the historian scorns such a superficial device. Rich and Cromwell are shown trying to incriminate More through the shabby device of the charge of embezzlement – the case of Catherine Anger in the Court of Requests. This, as indeed was inevitable, breaks down like a pack of cards. But the enemies of More are inflexible. As Cromwell grimly says, 'The King is not pleased with you.' He puts the matter even more plainly to his underling Rich when he says,

The King wants Sir Thomas More either to bless his marriage or to be destroyed. Either will do.

And since More has a conscience and will neither explicitly or implicitly 'bless' the marriage, then his destruction is a foregone conclusion. Every step in the sequence of events is as inevitable as if it had been planned with inescapable logic. We find More in the Tower and over him the rack hangs menacingly. Even the walls drip – it is hard to say whether from the river or from the blood of those who have paid for their 'treason' with their lives.

In a last moving scene Margaret and Alice try to persuade him. Margaret cries, 'Haven't you done as much as God can reasonably want?'; and Alice tries to jolt him into a sense of proportion when she declares, 'Are you content to be shut up here with mice and rats when you might have been at home with us?'

From that moment the descent into cruel tragedy is swift. There follows the trial, the perjury of Rich and the sentence. The last we see of More is when he turns to the Headsman and bids him not to be afraid of his office. 'You send me to God.'

More's wife and daughter are the only two named women in the play, and in the setting of a historical play of the sixteenth century their parts are necessarily small. Their presence gives variety in characterization and also throws More's integrity into greater relief. He is seen to plough a lone furrow at home as well as in matters of state. His wife and his favourite daughter (his family representatives in the play) plead with him to capitulate – but in vain. At home and in the world outside all are against him, and this throws into greater prominence More's honesty and bravery.

Alice, according to Bolt 'born into the merchant class', is something of a shrew, something of a snob; but she is warm-hearted and not without courage, as shown in the final episode in which she appears. But she is overdressed, coarse and uneducated: 'I'll bet . . . I see no falcon stoop from no cloud' (a misuse of language in which 1960 is clearly in evidence). Unable even to read, she seems to represent everything that More is not. He obviously loves her, however, and desperately seeks her understanding of his position. She in her turn, unable to comprehend his fine distinctions of dogma, can still understand that More is 'the best man that I ever met or am likely to'.

The Common Man

The master statesman of us all. 'I don't understand.'

The character of the Common Man has given rise to much critical discussion. One cause of the sudden popularity of historical plays during the 'sixties is undoubtedly the growing influence of Bertolt Brecht, the German director, poet and dramatist, whose influence has dominated the contemporary theatre of our age. Between 1937 and 1945 Brecht, a fugitive from Nazi Germany, wrote a series of plays, many of which are now recognized as masterpieces in their own right. Perhaps the greatest of these was the historical play *Galileo*. Brecht's influence has been felt in the European and American theatre in two ways. In the first place, all his work has a humanist and political awareness, and even at times a didactic note running through it. Brecht has frequently appeared as a theorist of the theatre, and it is probably not too much to say that his writings on the theatre have exerted as much influence as those of Stanislavsky.

But he was not merely a theorist. He was a practical man of the theatre and it was because of this that he was recognized as one of the greatest figures in the contemporary theatre. Particularly important has been his concept of the Alienation Effect. In brief, the idea behind this is that Brecht envisages the theatre, not as a place for the satisfaction of wish-fulfilment, but as a highly *critical* place, and he requires of actors and audience alike a critical detachment from the play and its performance. Brecht's theory first and foremost requires the dramatist and the actor to use a deliberate technique to keep the audience in a state of critical awareness. They must be constantly aware that they are acting *a play*; they must never forget that they are actors, they must never identify themselves with the characters they are portraying.

Robert Bolt in his Preface to the play has himself paid tribute to Brecht as a master mind whose influence on this play has been considerable.

In two previous plays, *Flowering Cherry* and *The Tiger and the Horse*, I had tried, but with fatal timidity, to handle contemporaries in a style that should make them larger than life . . . Inevitably these plays looked like what they most resembled. [Mr Bolt here alludes to the theory that the theatre is a house with a fourth wall removed, so exposing all private action to view.] The style I eventually used was a bastardized version of the one most recently associated with Bertolt Brecht.

Then Bolt goes on to explain that many people have obtained a wrong idea of Brecht's theories. They regard the Alienation Effect as something like a 'slap in the face'. They think that alienation terminates rather than deepens audience participation. This is not so.

Simply to slap your audience in the face satisfies an austere and puritanical streak which runs in many of his [Brecht's] disciples and sometimes, detrimentally I think, in Brecht himself. But it is a dangerous game to play . . . When we use alienation methods just for kicks we in the theatre are sawing through the branch on which we are sitting.

The most notorious of Brecht's alienation effects was the presence on the stage of a character who stood apart from the rest; here Brecht was only building on the work of his predecessors in the theatre. Both the French stage of Dumas and the theatre of Ibsen were perfectly familiar with the character of the 'Raisonneur', that is, a character who explains to the audience precisely what the problem is. Indeed perhaps the origin of the role goes back to Shakespearian times, when the First Gentleman, Second Gentleman and so on existed simply in order to reveal foregoing events. But Brecht's method is to use the character, not as a means of presenting explanatory material, but to address the audience direct, and so destroy the cosy illusion of naturalistic realism. Bolt's Common Man is a Brechtian character cut down to size. 'He is intended to draw the audience into the play, not thrust them off it.' But Bolt considers that he largely failed in this intention – and for this reason: 'The word "common" was intended primarily to indicate "that which is common to us all". But he was taken instead as ... that mythical beast The Man in The Street.'

The result was that the Common Man divided the audience, in a sense politically, into opponents and supporters of the principle of egalitarianism. Some spectators assumed that the Common Man *was* common – and regarded him as vulgar. By others the role was resented as an attempt to divide mankind into 'them' (representing the 'Establishment') and 'us'.

Actually the Common Man's chief contribution to the action of the play is that he proves invaluable in defining the various localities of episodes. Through the device of a wardrobe basket, containing appropriate costumes and 'properties', he takes the opportunity to paint the scene and comment briefly on the action. Thus, at the beginning of the play he assumes the character of More's steward Matthew, the arch-spokesman of common sense. From then on, throughout the play, he assumes a number of small supporting parts (boatman, gaoler, executioner) in which his attitude is that of ironic commentator – the one man who has no illusions – and in that way he constantly reminds the average audience of wordly-wise philosophy. His changes with the tide of circumstances, public opinion and private opportunity also serve to throw into relief the constant integrity of More.

The Duke

We're supposed to be the arrogant ones ... and we've all given in!

The Duke of Norfolk represents the aristocrats – the real rulers of the country. Thomas, the third Duke of Norfolk (1473–1554), a life-long opponent of Wolsey, might be taken as a symbol of the nobles' hatred of self-made men like Wolsey, who achieve power without the need for influence. Whereas Wolsey was a poor man's son, a fact that rankled in Norfolk's heart, Norfolk symbolized all that wealth and privilege offered. In effect he was one of the last representatives of the baronial class, of whom Henry VII had already disposed. Instead of turning to his class for running the country, Henry VIII put his trust in men like Wolsey and Cromwell, men without family connections, who therefore were committed exclusively to Henry's policies: they had been made by Henry, and were identified with his rule. They owed no allegiance to the Norfolks and their like, and that was why Norfolk displayed such a deep hatred of Wolsey, the archetype of statesmen who had taken over from the ruling families and threatened their existence.

These implacable enemies stood for opposite things; Norfolk's chief ambition was the ruin of Wolsey. And the hour of Wolsey's débâcle was the hour of Norfolk's triumph: a hollow one, for he did not succeed, as he had hoped, to Wolsey's fortunes. As President of the Privy Council he sought to supplant Wolsey in the counsels of the King, but since he lacked Wolsey's genius he clearly could be of no great political service to the King. Anne Boleyn was Norfolk's niece; he watched her rise and fall with equal nonchalance. He presided over the trial that resulted in her being attainted for treason. But he had good luck with other relatives – another niece, Catharine Howard, later became one of Henry's wives. Cromwell succeeded Wolsey as the real man of power, and Norfolk was merely a figure-head.

It is this aspect of Norfolk's character that Bolt has seized upon for theatrical representation. He is perhaps the nearest to a 'stock character' – says all the 'right' things and holds the proper opinions for one of the country's 'natural rulers' – a typical Establishment figure, who regards the country as his natural inheritance.

Thomas Cromwell

He must submit!

Bolt regards Thomas Cromwell as an intellectual bully. In the play, Cromwell had not then reached the pinnacle of his career – when for six years he was the unmistakable ruler of Tudor England: but already he both suggested and organized Henry's power. He is a rather terrifying figure; and Bolt sees him as something of a sadist, something of a power addict. He is vindictive (e.g. removing the books from More's prison cell) and sarcastic; the two qualities often go together. After the downfall of Cardinal Wolsey (because he failed to bring about the divorce), Henry found in Cromwell (1485–1544) a minister fitted to his ambition. Like Wolsey, Cromwell was a man of the humblest birth; and the first of his kind to attain the greatest power in the state. An utter absence of moral scruple gives colour to the suggestion that he was an earnest disciple of Machiavelli; indeed, in the play, it is he who recommends Rich to read Machiavelli. He is an expert in double-talk and slippery tactics. Efforts have been made by some historians to evaluate Cromwell as a Protestant martyr, in view of his end. But such distortions of history have little effect. As A. D. Innes (*Ten Tudor Statesmen*) has written, 'No playwright or novelist has made him a central figure in drama or novel. Yet it may seriously be argued that his personality was one which most decisively altered the course of history.'

Cromwell was a man of action. Quite clearly in public life he poured contempt on 'empty gabblers, who talked at large about everything under the sun while doing nothing'. He was the first of the anti-Parliamentarians – the first of the Fascists. He came to the notice of Wolsey, and his affairs prospered. While the toils of the divorce suit gradually wore Wolsey down, and eventually brought about his downfall, Cromwell waited for his hour to strike. He obtained the ear of the King: finance was the keynote to his success. He struck at the authority of the Pope through the wealthy monasteries. It was Cromwell who promoted the Supremacy Bill. Wolsey's death had proved most convenient; his successor was Cranmer, a sufficiently pliable tool without qualms of conscience.

In the play momentous events seem to occur with the inevitability of dates in a calendar. But in fact dates are not important here – though 1533 *is* crucial, in that it saw the irreversible breach with the Papacy. (It was not, however, until 1534 that Pope Clement issued judgement in favour of Catherine.) From that moment King Henry and Cromwell went ahead. The marriage with Anne Boleyn led to the Act of Succession. 'I pray that these things be not confirmed with oaths,' said More. But that is exactly what happened.

To force both More and John Fisher, the Bishop of Rochester, to acknowledge the Royal Supremacy in place of the Pope's would have been the supreme triumph. Nothing would have beaten down possible opposition so much as the winning over of such opponents. Cromwell drafted the Oath in such a way that there was no escaping by means of legal quibbles. More and Fisher refused to desert their principles. They would accept the succession as a pragmatic measure – a *fait accompli*; they would never take the Oath as prescribed.

It is important for the student to understand the exact position; in the theatre events take place so quickly that the audience has not always time to grasp the significance of the issues involved, and when this happens the play is less successful dramatically. Here the spectator might imagine that More and Fisher were making a mountain out of a molehill.

Nothing could be farther from the truth: both Cromwell and Henry were anxious to proceed according to the strict letter of the law. Yet it appeared that mere refusal to take the Oath – silence, malicious or otherwise – offered a defence; the omission was soon rectified. A new Treason Act was passed, in which it was expressly declared treason merely to question the titles of the Queen and her heirs, and silence was to be construed as treason.

It was this that brought More and Fisher within the net. If they remained firm, there was no escape from execution. We cannot be certain, but it is possible that, for the sake of happy days long past, Henry might have allowed More to spend his days in prison. But there is not the slightest shadow of doubt that Cromwell did not suffer a single qualm. The death sentence was made certain when the new Pope, who succeeded Clement, created Fisher a Cardinal. To Cromwell these men had been merely obstacles; to Henry they now appeared as implacable enemies. More's doom was sealed.

The Archbishop

Weigh a doubt against a certainty – and sign.

Thomas Cranmer (1489–1556) was a rather dim figure; against his will he was compelled to be a protagonist in a drama which he neither understood nor wanted. Few characters have aroused as much controversy as Cranmer, and Bolt, not surprisingly, has taken refuge in a rather conventional portrait of a stage figure instead of stating an original viewpoint. It is somewhat difficult to form any view of this rather colourless figure: certainly the stage Cranmer gives little sign of being the man who aroused such bitter controversy among his biographers.

Historically, every important action in Cranmer's life has had its defenders and its attackers. A very interesting character, he makes little impression in this play. That he held no strong views on the Papacy we may well believe. His career was undistinguished, in the sense that he apparently did little to deserve the greatness that was thrust upon him. Whereas More instantly made his mark, Cranmer spent twenty-five years in an inferior position at Cambridge. His chance came with 'the King's affair' – the great divorce. Cranmer made an original contribution to the theological question; and Henry thus discovered the man who 'had the sow by the right ear'. He distinguished himself as a propagandist for the King's cause, and – while staying at the house of Anne Boleyn's father – wrote a book on the divorce. As it transpired, Pope Clement gave an adverse judgement before Cranmer had an opportunity of raising the technical points involved in a consideration of the biblical books Deuteronomy and Leviticus.

By practice men become masters of intrigue. The Cambridge recluse in course of time became a cunning and skilful agent on behalf of his king. His connection with the Boleyn interest thrived; and he received his reward in 1533 when he was appointed Archbishop of Canterbury. (Incidentally, the precise chronology of the play is not always clear. Act I ended in 1530; Act II begins in May 1532. But the exact timing of each individual episode is left indefinite. It is not necessary, for a comprehension of the play, to allocate the date of these scenes exactly.)

Certainly Cranmer tried to persuade More that Catherine of Aragon's marriage was invalid. (More was Lord Chancellor until 1532, when he resigned.) Cranmer's appointment as Archbishop was unexpected, at any rate no one outside the royal circle knew of the high opinion that Henry had formed of him. The fact is that the powerful influence of the Boleyn family had been at work. But to the ordinary 'man in the street' it looked as though this was simple trading. Cranmer seemed to have said in effect, 'Make me Archbishop of Canterbury, and I will give you leave to be an adulterer.'

Although seemingly a somewhat colourless figure, Cranmer did, nevertheless, put his finger on one of the weaknesses of More's case. If More did not blame those who took the Oath of Supremacy, it *must* be that it was doubtful. In the case of doubt, he should have given the benefit to Henry. Cranmer's was the only argument that baffled More: he could think of no answer.

Richard Rich

Every man has his price!

Rich was an almost exact contemporary of Roper, and in the play represents the 'younger generation'. Although unfamiliar to all except students doing research in the Tudor period, Richard Rich was the typical turncoat, the man who benefits from kindness, then takes great pleasure in 'biting the hand that has fed him'. Practically all the men who played a great part in Henry's reign – Wolsey, More, Fisher, Cromwell, Somerset, Seymour – sooner or later went to the block. Rich, the Judas of English history, alone died safely in his bed.

The playwright has presented him as a 'studious unhappy academic, tortured by doubt, longing to be rescued from himself'. This would appear to be a very subjective interpretation, the actual Rich being a much more detestable figure – but one that every despotism throws up: the man who contrives to keep a safe skin while his betters go under.

He is introduced as a struggling barrister, a Cambridge man who is recommended to take up teaching – More is prepared to find him a post with Dr Colet of St Paul's. But Rich is only prepared to work for self-advancement. He therefore thinks it more expedient to fawn upon his social betters: More, Cromwell and Wolsey. His career began when he came to the notice of Wolsey: like many reactionaries in later life, he began by being a wholesale reformer who smelled out corruption in high places. In May 1532 he was made Attorney-General for Wales, the first of the plums of office that fell into his lap. The dramatist has used some licence in incorporating historical facts: in October 1533 Rich was knighted upon becoming Solicitor-General; and it was in this capacity that he took the leading part in More's prosecution for treason.

It was his perjured evidence that ultimately convicted More. Rich reaped the reward – he was loaded with money and honours. In one of his 'Establishment' speeches he once likened Henry VIII to a Solomon for justice, a Samson for strength and an Absalom for handsomeness; nor did he run out of metaphors there, for he added a Sun without which life could not exist. Next to Cromwell he was the most powerful of the 'Establishment' figures, but with this difference: he always managed to be on the winning side, in spite of the many changes of mood and policy of his master Henry.

When Cromwell too fell on evil times, Rich deserted him; repeating the pattern of his perjury in the More trial, he turned against Cromwell at the last, in what Froude described as 'the darkest page in England's history'. It has been said that 'The roll of martyrs in England was due to Rich's persecution.'

Historically, Rich's only act of benevolence was the founding of Felsted public school. Rich is revealed in the play to be a typical instrument of tyranny, the pliant and willing instrument, a type of which the world has had many examples over the years. His perjured character throws More's integrity into strong dramatic relief. It was More's individual integrity, coupled with Rich's perjury, that sent More to his death.

William Roper

Nice boy . . . Terribly strong principles though.

William Roper was the son-in-law of Sir Thomas More, who married More's daughter Margaret (by his first wife.) He is envisaged in this play as a man in the early thirties – a man of little imagination, but filled with rectitude and principle: he was historically the first biographer of the saint of 'clear and unspotted conscience'. He was continually resident in More's household and it is largely through his *Life* that we know more of More's family, his background and personal environment than is usual in the case of great men. The play undoubtedly owes a great deal

to Roper's biography, which must have been one of the dramatist's primary sources.

Roper is first introduced to the audience as a suitor for the
hand of Margaret, though More is, at the beginning, against the
proposed marriage. With Rich, Roper represents the younger
generation (a better specimen); like Rich he has been reading
for the bar, and when he enters the play he is about to be called.
As More says, the Ropers were barristers when the Mores were
selling pewter: More's objection to Roper as a son-in-law is not
based on family fortune; it is simply that Roper is a heretic, a
Lutheran. More is determined that until Roper changes his
ideas he shall not marry Margaret. As it happens, Roper changes
his allegiance; and when Henry attacks the Church, Roper in his
idealism supports the Pope. He says to Margaret, 'I'm not a
convenient man, Meg – I've got an inconvenient conscience!'
More laughingly likens him to Joshua's trumpet: 'One note on
that brass conscience of yours and my daughter's walls are
down.' He clearly is no time-server: he is not afraid to tell More
to his face that 'The Court has corrupted you, Sir Thomas; you
are not the man you were; you have learnt to study your "con-
venience"; you have learnt to flatter!'

Roper is not a 'trimmer' – he will not win Margaret by sacrifi-
cing his independence. In this respect he is a complete foil to
Rich. And there is a brief, but valuable scene of confrontation
between Roper and Rich in which Roper is quick to detect Rich's
defection (Act I, p.37).

In certain respects he seems more alive to the dangers of
More's position than More himself. At any rate he realizes earlier than More the logical consequences of Henry's Act of Supremacy. He cuts through the legal mumbo-jumbo, and predicts
that the legal quibble on which More is at first content to rely will
prove useless. Like many a man of strong principle he is a
nuisance to those around him, a constant reminder of what is
pure and holy – he will not be discreet. Yet when Alice is
resentful at More's refusal to keep in with the powers that be, it
is to Roper that he turns for comfort (Act II, p.55).

Roper is inclined to frown on More's habit of self-mockery at
important moments: 'While we are witty,' he says quietly, 'the
Devil may enter us unawares.' It is Roper who brings the information that there is to be a new Act of Parliament requiring
everyone to take an Oath, failure to take which is to be construed

as treason. More is quick to ask, 'But what is the wording?' Roper contemptuously replies they are concerned with meanings, not words. But More, anxious to find a place to rest a possible defence, says that an oath consists of words. Here one feels that Roper was right in the larger sense; he is not to be put off by narrow legalistic arguments.

The King

I'll have no opposition!

It is important to realize that this play is about More, not primarily about Henry VIII. This king has passed into the mythology of the English race, and he is remembered in history as a gross sensualist who combined insatiable tyranny and bestial appetites in about equal proportions.

In the play he is important as the dictator whose actions and policy (carried out by his underlings) are responsible for More's dilemma. Henry appears only in one scene. In this he appears not as the overfed, outsize man of Holbein's portrait, but rather as a young king – always talking about himself; delighted as a ten-year-old to get his shoes muddy; unwarrantably proud of his skill in dancing and wrestling and of his flimsy artistic accomplishments ('we artists'). He is very well satisfied that he is in a position to command better men than himself; and loses his temper as soon as he is crossed.

Henry is not altogether pleased when his knowledge of Latin is surpassed. Although pleased to be commended as a writer, when his ability in Latin is shown to be secondary he petulantly deprecates books and learning by quoting a Bible tag. In all accomplishments he shall be the first. However, he soon recovers to announce to Margaret that 'I'm something of a scholar too'. He likes people to hang on his words and goes on talking of what he has been doing even while music is playing and when he has commanded More to listen to it ('*Listen*, man, *listen*'). 'I launched a ship today, Thomas,' he goes on, quite certain that he will have no competition in conversation. His own selfish nature as an absolute monarch, coupled with other people's flattery, has made him into a contemptible character; and this leads on to the final scene of the play.

General questions plus questions on related topics for coursework/examinations on other books you may be studying

1 What would you say was the theme of this play? Illustrate fully.

Suggested notes for essay answer:
(a) Since More is the most important character, a brief indication of the plot, the historical treatment by Bolt, and the situation More faces should be in the Introduction. (b) Theme is integrity, which involves honesty, self-sacrifice, passive resistance, keeping word and faith, etc. The answer must cover the range of the play, and could deal with More's display of integrity in Act I first; examples are conversation with Rich (More does not accept that everyone has his price); with Wolsey (More won't support King's divorce) and the King's visit (More won't go along with his wishes). (c) Concentrate on Act II – removal of chain of office; accepts reduction of household – deals with Spanish ambassador – withstands Cromwell – imprisonment – refusal to take new oath. (d) Conclusion: More – State/Church – examples of reasoning – puts honour before expediency etc. Quote from text. Put in some quotations which illustrate the theme – if necessary link with sub-themes.

2 Analyse the construction of *A Man for All Seasons* episode by episode.

3 Give examples of the way in which the playwright suggests the social background of the period.

4 'Since the subject is integrity, the play aims high.' Discuss this statement.

5 The role of the Common Man attracted a great deal of critical attention when the play was first produced. What is the importance of the part?

6 'The presence of a Chorus always weakens the dramatic effect of a play.' Would you say that this was true in the case of the Common Man?

7 In the epigraph to *A Man for All Seasons* Bolt quotes the following: 'More is a man of an angel's wit . . . a man of marvellous mirth.' Give examples of this 'mirth' from the play.

8 One dramatic critic entitled his review of the play 'Chronicle of a Reluctant Hero'. How far would you agree with this description of More in the play?

9 What is the significance of the title? How far does the play reveal More to be 'a man for all seasons'?

10 Give a brief character-sketch of Norfolk and discuss his importance in the play.

11 Discuss the part played by Henry VIII in the play, in person and behind the scenes.

12 Of the two women characters, Alice and Margaret, which do you consider the more significant, and why?

13 'The characters talk and feel like twentieth-century people, although they are supposed to be sixteenth-century.' How far do you find this true?

14 'The dramatist should not take sides; his function is not to judge or condemn.' What is your opinion of this, and how far is *A Man for All Seasons* an illustration of it?

15 'A skilfully written play, but tame.' Do you agree?

16 In *A Man for All Seasons* how far is Robert Bolt indebted to or influenced by Brecht?

17 'As a figure for the superhuman context I took the largest, most alien, least formulated thing I know, the sea and water.' Give instances of this imagery, stating the context in each case.

18 Anachronisms often occur in historical plays. Give some instances in this play of the *deliberate* use of anachronism and say what you take to be its purpose.

19 Write about any novel or play you have read where the leading character is outstanding in his or her moral influence.

20 Give an account of a struggle for power in your chosen book.

21 Show how a wife helps her husband in any book you have read recently.

22 Write an essay on the author's use of history in one of your texts for study.

23 Consider the part played by betrayal or deception in your chosen book.

24 Write about any book you have studied where the presentation of religion or the law is important.

25 Show how any one character in the play or book you are studying engages your sympathies. Say why this is, and write a character-study of him/her.

26 Write a short story or brief dialogue in which one character gets the best of an argument.

Brodie's Notes

D. H. Lawrence	**The Rainbow**
D. H. Lawrence	**Sons and Lovers**
D. H. Lawrence	**Women in Love**
Harper Lee	**To Kill a Mockingbird**
Laurie Lee	**Cider with Rosie**
Christopher Marlowe	**Dr Faustus**
Arthur Miller	**The Crucible**
Arthur Miller	**Death of a Salesman**
John Milton	**Paradise Lost, Books I and II**
Robert C. O'Brien	**Z for Zachariah**
Sean O'Casey	**Juno and the Paycock**
George Orwell	**Animal Farm**
George Orwell	**1984**
J. B. Priestley	**An Inspector Calls**
J. D. Salinger	**The Catcher in the Rye**
William Shakespeare	**Antony and Cleopatra**
William Shakespeare	**As You Like It**
William Shakespeare	**Hamlet**
William Shakespeare	**Henry IV Part I**
William Shakespeare	**Henry IV Part II**
William Shakespeare	**Julius Caesar**
William Shakespeare	**King Lear**
William Shakespeare	**Macbeth**
William Shakespeare	**Measure for Measure**
William Shakespeare	**The Merchant of Venice**
William Shakespeare	**A Midsummer Night's Dream**
William Shakespeare	**Much Ado about Nothing**
William Shakespeare	**Othello**
William Shakespeare	**Richard II**
William Shakespeare	**Richard III**
William Shakespeare	**Romeo and Juliet**
William Shakespeare	**The Tempest**
William Shakespeare	**Twelfth Night**
George Bernard Shaw	**Arms and the Man**
George Bernard Shaw	**Pygmalion**
Alan Sillitoe	**Selected Fiction**
John Steinbeck	**Of Mice and Men** and **The Pearl**
Jonathan Swift	**Gulliver's Travels**
J. M. Synge	**The Playboy of the Western World**
Dylan Thomas	**Under Milk Wood**
Alice Walker	**The Color Purple**
Virginia Woolf	**To the Lighthouse**
W. B. Yeats	**Selected Poetry**

ENGLISH COURSEWORK BOOKS

Terri Apter	**Women and Society**
Kevin Dowling	**Drama and Poetry**
Philip Gooden	**Conflict**
Philip Gooden	**Science Fiction**
Margaret K. Gray	**Modern Drama**
Graham Handley	**Modern Poetry**
Graham Handley	**Prose**
Graham Handley	**Childhood and Adolescence**
R. J. Sims	**The Short Story**